SARA STONE | ANDY YURA
ILLUSTRATOR

Lily and the Snow
Copyright @ 2023
Sara Stone

Illustrated by Andy Yura
Layout by Fresh Design

Published in Canada
ISBN 978-1-7389600-0-2 softcover
ISBN 978-1-7389600-1-9 hardcover

www.sstonebooks.com

All Rights Reserved. No part of this book can be scanned, distributed, or copied without permission. This book or any portion thereof may not be reproduced or used in any manner whatsoever without the express written permission of the publisher—except for the use of brief quotations in a book review.

Dear Parents, Guardians, and Educators,

From a very young age, we noticed that our child was being triggered by daily activities and having strong reactions to them. She found many everyday experiences upsetting, like washing hands, bath time, loud sounds, and unfamiliar places. For the longest time, her father and I struggled to understand what was going on and support her.

Thankfully, after we sought professional help, our frustration and confusion gave way to insight. Over the years, we saw a pediatrician, physiotherapist, neurologist, psychologist, and occupational therapist to find answers. For parents of neurodivergent (ND) children, it can be quite a journey!

As they say, knowledge is power, and with knowledge in hand, developing strategies can lead to success. I hope this book can provide awareness of Sensory Processing Disorder (SPD) through examples of what it can be like for those who live with it.

Every child is unique, and the scenarios described in this book will not reflect the experiences of every child with SPD. But I hope this book has provided a springboard for further learning and understanding.

If you or a child in your care is affected by SPD, I encourage you to seek out the support of healthcare professionals. These include occupational therapists, neuropsychologists, and pediatric psychologists.

With the right kind of support and understanding, children and adults with SPD can lead fulfilling, joyful, and successful lives.

Warmly, Sara Stone

P.S. The same Lily from this story is now the first to suggest sledding after a snowfall! There are surprising possibilities ahead!

Once there was a girl named Lily who was **SMART, FUNNY, SWEET, AND STRONG.** She liked frogs, bedtime stories, and ice cream. But there was one thing she didn't like, not one bit - **SNOW!**

While the neighborhood kids were sledding down hills, building snow forts, and playing snow games outside, Lily would stay indoors.

"I don't like the feeling or the sound of snow crunching under my feet," Lily told her mom. "It makes me very uncomfortable."

Whenever it snowed, Lily and her parents would see the other children throwing snowballs, making snow angels, and even building frog snowmen. But Lily never wanted to play in the snow with them.

Lily's parents could see how much fun the other kids had in the snow. They told Lily how much they wished she would change her mind and join in.

But she never did— because the sound and the feeling of walking in the snow bothered her so much.

One day, the warm sunshine melted the snow into slushy piles. Soon, the road was clear of snow and wet with squishy puddles. Everyone knew how much Lily loved to splash in puddles after the rain.

Her mom suggested that they explore the slush together. And Lily agreed! So, they put on their hats, coats, gloves, and boots to go outside.

Slowly and carefully, Lily put the toe of her right boot into the nearest slush pile.

SPLOOSH!

went the slush. "Hmmm," thought Lily: This melted snow doesn't crunch under my feet.

SPLOOSH!
went the slush again,
under her left boot.

SPLASH!

SPLISH!

SPLOOSH!

Lily and her mom stomped down the road—stopping at each slush pile along the way. Lily started at one end of the road—stomping and splashing her way to the end of the street.

She was grinning in the sunshine while fully enjoying her wet winter adventure.

Lily and her mom came indoors just as the snow began to fall again.

They warmed up with tea and cookies as they looked through the window to watch the falling snow.

"I don't like the snow," Lily told her mom as she sipped her tea.

"You do like the slush, though, don't you?" asked her mother.

Lily remembered enjoying the wet, cold slush splashing under her boots and replied,

"YES, I DO LIKE SLUSH."

"Well, that's something to appreciate!" said her mom with a smile. "And spring is just around the corner!"

Yes, thought Lily, I love spring best of all!
There are so many rain puddles. And I can't
wait to see some new baby frogs by the pond!

Then, she thought: On a warm spring day,
we might have a picnic at the frog pond . . .
And get ice cream for dessert.

NOW, THAT WOULD BE FUN!

What is Sensory Processing Disorder?

Sensory processing disorder (SPD) is a condition that affects how a person's brain processes sensory information (also called stimuli). Sensory processing includes receiving, processing, and responding to sensory input from one's body and the environment. Sensory information includes what a person sees, hears, tastes, smells, or touches. It also includes how they perceive their own body positions and movements.

SPD can affect one or more of a person's senses or all of them. Having SPD often means a person is overly sensitive or under-sensitive to stimuli when most other people are not. This can lead a person with SPD to struggle with daily activities, social interactions, and emotional regulation. They can also experience problems with motor coordination, task organization, and self-regulation (which includes self-control). SPD is typically identified and treated by occupational therapists and other healthcare professionals.

For more information about SPD, please check out the links below:

https://sensoryhealth.org/basic/understanding-sensory-processing-disorder

https://childmind.org/article/sensory-processing-issues-explained/

Some helpful book resources are;

'Raising A Sensory Smart Child'
by Lindsey Biel and Nancy Peske

'The Sensory-Sensitive Child'
by Karen Smith PhD and Karen Grouze PhD

'The Goodenoughs Get in Sync:
Family Members Overcome Their Special Sensory Issues'
by Carol Stock Kranowitz

'The Out-of-Sync Child, Third Edition'
by Carol Stock Kranowitz

Please check out your local library or online
for more informative books on SPD.

SARA STONE is an author, educator, and teacher-librarian who resides on beautiful Vancouver Island, Canada. She is an avid reader with a lifelong love of children's literature.

When she's not writing, Sara loves reading in the company of her lap dog, Cookie, chatting at book club, or drawing with her creative daughter and talented husband. She is passionate about using storytelling to inspire and educate, and she is thrilled to have the opportunity to do just that with her debut picture book!

Sara hopes that readers will love and be inspired by the story of **Lily and the Snow** as much as she has loved creating it!

www.sstonebooks.com

www.ingramcontent.com/pod-product-compliance
Lightning Source LLC
Chambersburg PA
CBHW041703160426
43209CB00017B/1735